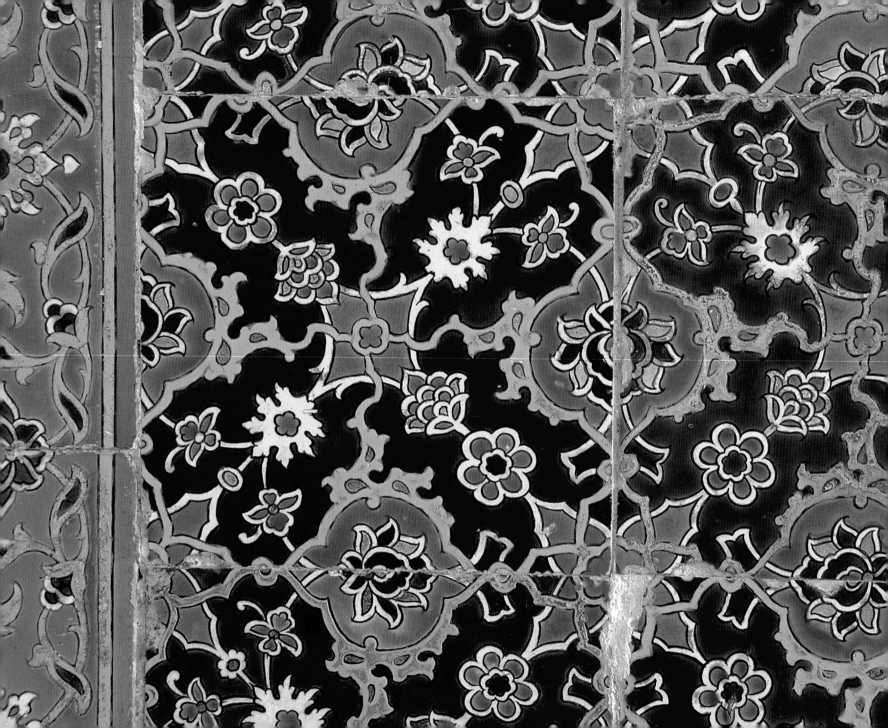

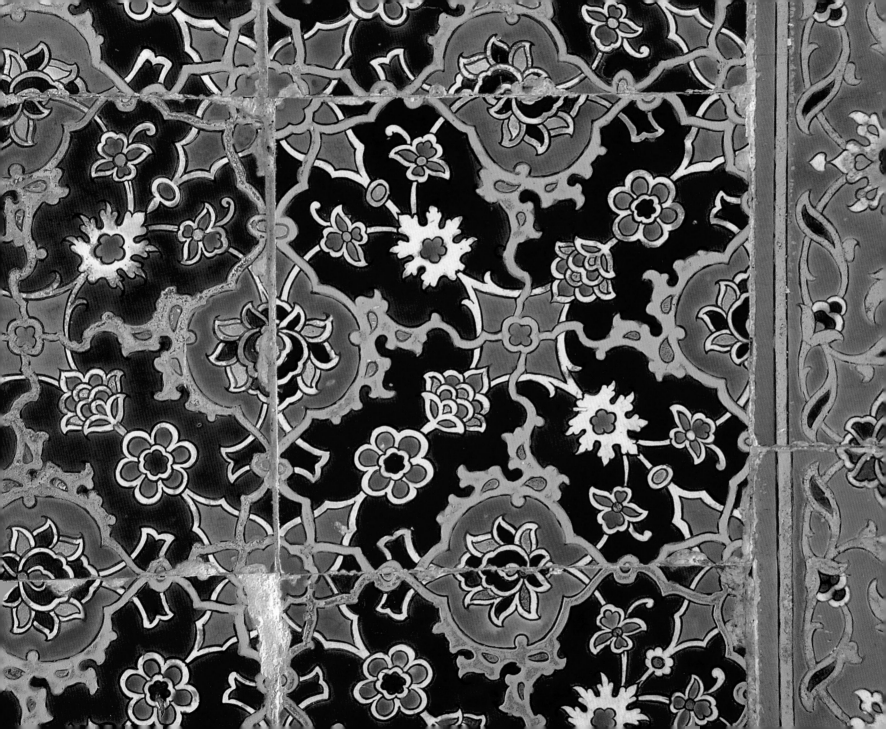

For Nurten Yoruk who helped write this book,
Suleyman Tank for his support, and my family Pyper, Topaloğlu,
Adan, Guney and Dassargiris – N.T.P.

For the Mayor of Sivas who helped me get close to the country, Janetta, Judith
and Yvonne for their continued faith in me, and the many children of Turkey
who shared my enthusiasm – P.D.

T is for Turkey copyright © Frances Lincoln Limited 2010
Text copyright © Nilüfer Topaloğlu Pyper 2010
Photographs copyright © Prodeepta Das 2010
The Publishers wish to acknowledge Ifeoma Onyefulu as the originator
of the series of which this book forms a part.
Ifeoma Onyefulu is the author and photographer of *A is for Africa*.

First published in Great Britain and in the USA in 2010 by
Frances Lincoln Children's Books.
The Quarto Group, The Old Brewery, 6 Blundell Street, London N7 9BH, United Kingdom.
T (0)20 7700 6700 F (0)20 7700 8066
www.Quarto.com

British Library Cataloguing in Publication Data
available on request

ISBN: 978-0-7112-6116-7

Set in Romic

Printed in China
5 7 9 8 6 4

T is for Turkey

Nilüfer Topaloğlu Pyper

Prodeepta Das

F

FRANCES LINCOLN
CHILDREN'S BOOKS

Author's note

Turkey is a huge country which straddles two continents, Europe and Asia, divided by a narrow strip of water called the Bosphorus. It is bordered by the Aegean Sea, the Black Sea and the Mediterranean, and has its own inland sea — the Marmara. We have so many mountains, rivers and forests that we can enjoy all four seasons at the same time. When some of us are skiing in Erzurum, others are swimming in Antalya!

Turkey has a great history and its Ottoman Empire once spread into three continents. In Istanbul you can see the Blue Mosque, the Topkapi Palace, the Grand Bazaar and many famous mosques, churches and synagogues.

We also have some of the most delicious cooking in the world and each region has its own specialities.

Children have a special place in our lives. The founder of our modern republic, Atatürk, dedicated 23rd April to the children of Turkey, and we celebrate it every year as a national holiday.

Turkish people are friendly, generous and hospitable and I am proud to be part of such a beautiful country.

Aa

is for Atatürk. Mustafa Kemal Atatürk, known as the Father of the Turks, founded the modern Republic of Turkey in 1923. A brave leader who wanted peace in the world, he became the first President of Turkey, creating western laws and making Ankara our capital city.

 is for Bezirganbaşi, a traditional children's game. The players stand in a line, chanting rhymes. Then they walk under the arched arms of a pair of children, taking one side or the other. The game ends with a lively tug-of-war between the two sides.

C c

is for Çay (pronounced *chy*).
Black tea is our most popular
drink. We drink it from a
small, thin glass on a saucer,
sometimes with a slice
of lemon. Çay is mainly
produced in the Black Sea
region. There are tea gardens
everywhere for families to sit
in and enjoy their tea.

 **D**d is for Dolmuş (pronounced *dolmoosh*), a minibus which is our main form of public transport. Each dolmuş seats up to 15 people, with room for others to stand (*dolmuş* means "stuffed"). Many dolmuş drivers listen to music as they drive, so travelling by dolmuş is sometimes noisy!

Ee is for Ephesus, on the Aegean coast. Ephesus was once the Roman capital of Asia. Its Temple of Artemis was one of the Seven Wonders of the Ancient World, and up on Nightingale Mountain the Virgin Mary is said to have spent the last part of her life. People from all over the world come to see the temple, pay their respects and pray.

 **F f**

F is for Figs. Turkey is one of the world's main exporters of figs. Most figs are grown on the Aegean coast. Sweet, juicy and ready to eat, they are bursting with vitamins and minerals. They taste delicious fresh or dried, and are perfect for making jam.

 **g** is for Grandparents. They are an important part of our family and take a big part in looking after us. Whenever we see one of our grandparents, we kiss their hand and hold it to our forehead, to show our respect. On special occasions and at religious festivals we always visit them first, before we see anyone else.

 **h** is for Henna Night, a women-only party that takes place the night before a wedding. The bride-to-be wears a beautiful dress and red veil. Her closest friends and family gather to eat, sing and dance. They put henna on their hands, and the stain stays there for weeks afterwards. For the bride it is a very emotional evening, because it is her last night living at her parents' house.

 **i** is for Ice Cream. We have a special, smooth ice cream called *maraş*, made from milk, sugar and *salep* (a kind of spice). As it freezes, it becomes hard, chewy and elastic. Sometimes we have to use a knife and fork to cut it!

 **j** is for Jam. Jam for breakfast is a must. Our mothers make jam from all kinds of fruit and vegetables, especially oranges, water melons, figs, aubergines – even roses.

Kk

is for Kangal Dog, also known as the Anatolian Dog, from central Turkey. Legends say that the original dog was bred from a lion crossed with a tiger! These black-faced dogs are famous for their strength and bravery and are prized by shepherds for their loyalty.

Ll

is for Leblebi, a snack made from chickpeas that we love to eat. You can buy it sweetened, red and spicy, yellow-roasted or white-roasted. Children often try to whistle with powdered leblebi in their mouths!

 **M m** is for Mevlana, a whirling dervish. Wearing specal robes and hats, dervishes perform a traditional dance called *sema* to Sufi music. Sufis believe in peace, tolerance and love, and their doors are open to people of all nationalities and faiths. A Mevlana festival is held every year in the Sufi centre at Konya.

 **N n** is for Nazar Boncuk, a bead used as a charm to ward off the Evil Eye. Each bead is made from blue glass, pottery or china painted with an eye. We pin them to the clothes of newborn babies. Some people keep them in their cars and homes, or wear them as jewellery.

 **o** is for Olive. Did you know that Turkey is one of the biggest olive-growers in the world? We eat olives for breakfast with cucumber, tomato, feta cheese, bread and sometimes *sucuk* (Turkish sausage).

 **P p** is for Pamukkale, which means "cotton castle", one of the world's natural wonders. It is a hot spring (35 °C) with white calcified chalk which forms steps and stalactites. Since Ancient Greek times people have been coming to Pamukkale to bathe and be cured of their ailments.

 **q**

is for Qu'ran, the Muslim holy book.
(It is spelt *Kuran* in Turkish.) Most
households own a copy of the Qu'ran
which is kept in a special place. Islam
is the main religion in Turkey, but
there are many Christians and Jews
too, and everyone respects everyone
else's religion.

 **R** r

is for Roses. Isparta in western Turkey is famous for its rose gardens. Roses are used for making skin cream, soap, oil, perfume and Turkish delight. Rosewater cologne is used in traditional ceremonies and as a food essence.

 **S** s

is for Simit, a favourite snack. It is round, made of flour and eggs and smothered in sesame seeds. We eat it with cheese when we are drinking çay. You will often see simit-sellers in the city streets.

 **T t** is for Turkey, a country bridging the two great continents of Europe and Asia. With a history going back 4,000 years, it has been a homeland to many civilisations, from ancient Hittites to modern Turkey. Nowadays everyone speaks the same language – Turkish. Our country has magnificent mountains, lakes, forests and seas, sunny weather all year round and fabulous food – which make it a heaven on Earth!

 u

is for Uniform. All school children wear a uniform, and it makes them look extremely smart walking to and from school. Buying a uniform is a special occasion for every child going to school for the first time.

 v is for Van Cat. The Van Cat comes from Lake Van in eastern Turkey. Unlike other cats, it loves water and likes to swim, and it has eyes which are different colours! Its fur is creamy-white or auburn-white and it grows much bigger than other kinds of cat.

 **W** is for Wrestling. Oil wrestling is popular in Turkey, and the wrestlers are called *pehlivan,* which means "strong man". Professional wrestlers wear tight leather trousers and cover their bodies with oil, making it difficult to grab and pin each other to the ground. The winner of each contest receives a golden belt.

 x

(like Q and W) is not part of the Turkish alphabet. Our alphabet has 29 letters. Each letter has a different sound, so it is easy to pronounce Turkish words.

 y

is for Yogurt. We like it mixed with garlic and cucumber and call it *cacik*. With water and salt added, it makes a refreshing drink known as *ayran*.

 **z**

Z is for Zurna, a traditional musical instrument. It looks like a flute but has a very special sound. At celebrations you will always see someone playing a zurna, while someone else plays the drum.

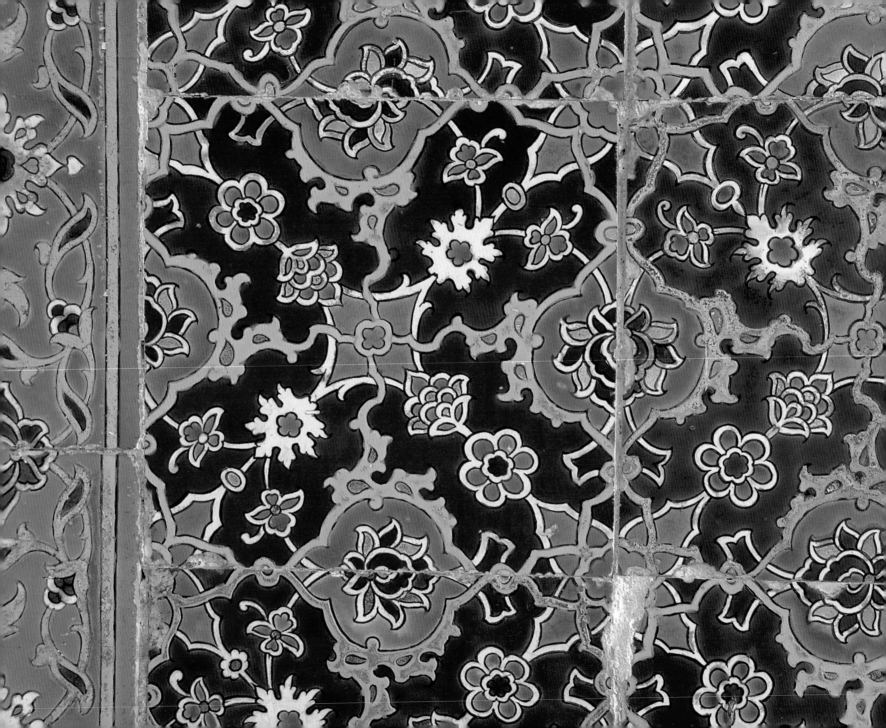

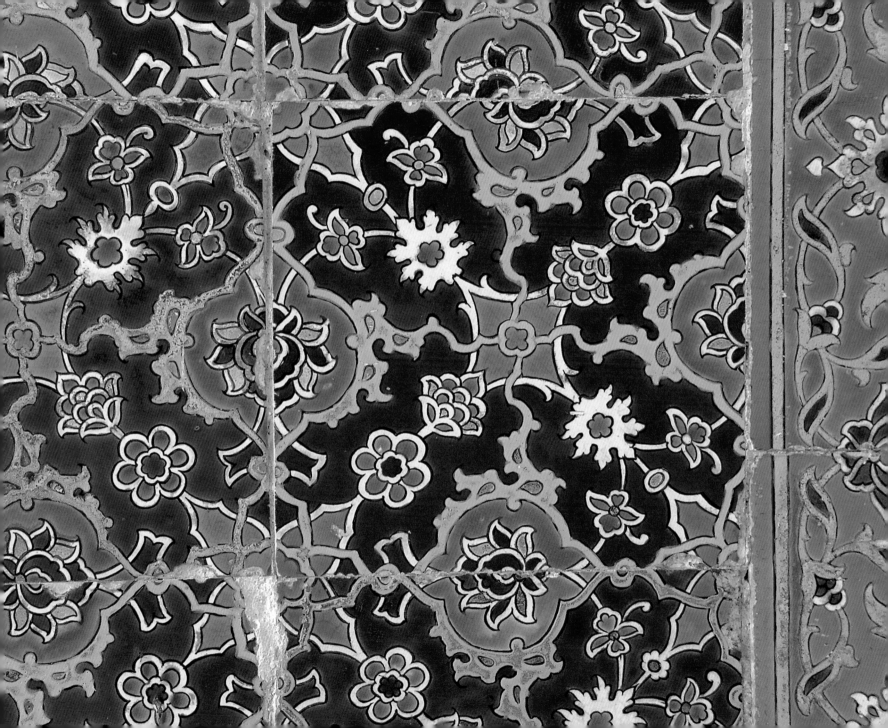